WHEN
THE
STARS
COME
OUT

For Kryshna, who has
walked with me through
the darkest of nights
~N.E.

For Mick and Hilary
~L.C.

A WORLD OF CHANGE?
The world is an ever-changing place, as you will discover. Our understanding of it is evolving, too.
New discoveries are there to be made, and new records may replace old ones.
We will be happy to revise and update information in future editions.

360 DEGREES, an imprint of Tiger Tales
5 River Road, Suite 128, Wilton, CT 06897
Published in the United States 2019
Originally published in Great Britain 2019
by Little Tiger Press Ltd.
Text by Nicola Edwards
Text copyright © 2019 Caterpillar Books
Illustrations copyright © 2019 Lucy Cartwright
ISBN-13: 978-1-944530-23-5
ISBN-10: 1-944530-23-1
Printed in China
CPB/1800/0964/0918

For more insight and activities, visit us at www.tigertalesbooks.com

WHEN THE STARS COME OUT

BY
NICOLA EDWARDS

ILLUSTRATED BY
LUCY CARTWRIGHT

HOW DOES THE NIGHT WORK?

It's always nighttime somewhere in the world. That's because our Earth, just like the other planets in our solar system, is constantly orbiting the Sun, which is the source of our light. It takes the Earth 24 hours to make one complete rotation on its axis, which makes each Earth day 24 hours long. As the Earth turns, half of it is facing the Sun at any one time, making it daytime in that half, and the other half is turned away from the Sun, making it nighttime in that half.

Although nighttime can be defined by a lack of sunlight on the patch of earth we live on, it is so much more than that. It is the realm of the Moon and stars, witches and ghosts, dreams and nightmares, magic and madness. It is a world in which we humans sleep, but many other creatures come to life.

For those who struggle to sleep, the night might seem a lonely place, but it holds a huge amount of activity and wonder if we dare to take a look. So let's begin....

SUNSET
(West)

SUNRISE
(East)

SUNRISE AND SUNSET
If we look up to the sky over the course of the day, we'll notice that the Sun seems to be moving across the sky. This is actually the Earth turning across the Sun's path. Each morning the Sun "rises" in the East, because the Earth is always spinning in the same direction, and then "sets" in the West. However, the Sun hasn't actually moved from East to West; it is our planet that has spun from West to East!

SPINNING SKIES

Even though we can't see the Sun at night, the Earth keeps spinning, which means that if we looked up at the sky over the course of the night, we'd see the stars seemingly move from East to West, just like the Sun appears to do during the day.

SUN

SUNLIGHT

EARTH

DAYTIME

NIGHTTIME

HISTORY OF THE NIGHT

The night has always been a world of darkness and the unknown, but an endlessly fascinating one, and our desire to understand the night can be seen as far back as the Bronze Age (3300–1200 BC). Ancient civilizations like the Harappans, Mayans, and Ancient Chinese all used the stars to track time and position their cities, and they also believed that astronomy (the study of the stars and other space objects) could predict the future.

WHO'S ORBITING WHOM?

Nicolaus Copernicus (1473–1543) argued that the Earth orbits the Sun, rather than the other way around. This caused an uproar at the time. Then, in 1610, Italian astronomer Galileo Galilei first observed the night sky through a telescope and saw that Jupiter had four moons orbiting it. This proved that not everything in the solar system revolved around the Sun.

MAPPING THE STARS

The Ancient Greeks named the stars and mapped their positions. Middle Eastern astronomers translated and continued this work, while Europe plunged into the Dark Ages (476–1000 AD), when there wasn't much stargazing going on!

TO INFINITY AND BEYOND

As science and technology have moved on, our understanding of the night sky has grown and grown, but even in the 1920s, astronomers were still unsure whether other galaxies were just clouds of dust and gas or whether they were entire "island universes" made of billions of stars.

We only found the first planets outside our solar system in 1992, and we still don't know how many stars there are out there in the universe, but our plans to conquer and understand the night sky continue.

LIFE ON MARS

NASA has announced its plans to land humans on Mars in the 2030s. Meanwhile, the Hubble Space Telescope (which weighs as much as two elephants and is a far cry from Galileo's hollow tube with lenses) continues to orbit the Earth, giving us crystal-clear, colorful images of exploding stars, whirlpool galaxies, and even the moments of a star's birth in clouds of gas and dust.

Compared to early humans, our knowledge of the night sky these days is impressive, but the dark reaches of space are vast and will probably always hold on to at least some of their mystery.

THE
SKY
AT NIGHT

"I have loved the stars too fondly to be fearful of the night."

— Sarah Williams

As our Sun disappears below the horizon, a blanket of darkness falls — but the night sky is far from a desolate place. We might see the Moon shining brightly or partly shrouded in atmospheric clouds. Maybe a carpet of twinkling stars or the majesty of the entire Milky Way stretches above us. Perhaps we'll be treated to the colorful dance of an aurora, a sparkling meteor shower, or an eerie moonbow.

Even when the night sky is starless, we might find ourselves entranced by a valley of twinkling city lights that brighten our view, or be drawn to the glow of a home's inviting windows, impossibly cozy against the darkness. Yes, even the blackest canvas of night has its own special magic....

VAMPIRES

These famous mythical creatures are said to feed on human blood. They like to sleep in coffins and only come out at night, as sunlight is poisonous to them. Garlic is said to keep them at bay.

ARE YOU AFRAID OF THE DARK?

ASWANGS

These Filipino legends look like normal people during the day, but when night comes, they shapeshift into crows, black dogs, or bats with bloodshot eyes. They find babies and small children particularly tasty, but they can be defeated in various ways, including by being whipped with a stingray's tail!

GHOULS

According to various folktales, these unsavory characters hang around in dark graveyards at night, eat the dead, and then take on the form of the last person they ate.

WEREWOLVES

These legendary night-dwellers look like humans during the day, but when the Sun sets and the Moon is full, they turn into hairy, scary, aggressive wolves. A cloudy sky is said to damp down their temper, but you still wouldn't want to meet one in a forest at night.

AMAROKS

These enormous wolves are part of Inuit mythology. They walk alone and stalk any human who is foolish enough to hunt solo at nighttime.

Are you afraid of the dark? Many people are, at least a little bit. It's part of human nature. That's because in earlier times, before we had fortress-like houses to sleep in, and electric lights to light up the darkness, we were easy prey for hunting animals with better night vision and a better sense of smell than us.

In those times, the best hope of safety at night was to sleep around the campfire with your tribe, just like you might do if you were out camping in the woods for fun!

You might keep a couple of lookouts awake, watching for signs of animals approaching from the darkness beyond. In some parts of the world, this is still the safest sleeping strategy!

Though many of us can now lock our doors and sleep soundly behind them until morning, the most primitive part of our brains is still wired to see threats lurking in the darkness. Some of these have become the stuff of legend….

SAFER NIGHTS

Whether it's mythical monsters, wild animals, unfriendly humans, or even just unseen natural hazards we fear stumbling into in the dark, we've always tried to light up our nights in one way or another.

• Historians believe our ancestors could have been controlling fire as far back as 400,000 years ago.

• Our first lamps came about around 70000 BC. They were made of shells or hollow rocks filled with animal fat, with a piece of moss that would act like a modern candlewick.

• Around 270 BC, the world's first known lighthouse, the Pharos lighthouse in Ancient Egypt, was built to guide boats safely into shore at night. This impressive structure was the second-tallest building in the world, after the Great Pyramid of Giza.

• In 1933, Englishman Percy Shaw was driving home at night along dangerous pitch-black roads when his headlights picked up the eyes of a cat on a fence. He realized night driving would be safer if glass reflectors were used as road markers and turned this brainstorm into a business. Now glass cat's eyes are used to light up dark roads all over the world!

"ONE GIANT LEAP"

In the 1950s and '60s, the world watched as two powerful countries, the United States and the USSR, competed against each other in a space race. When the Russians launched the first human, Yuri Gagarin, into space in 1961, American President John F. Kennedy became utterly determined to see U.S. astronauts land on the Moon before their rivals.

On July 16, 1969, Neil Armstrong, Buzz Aldrin, and Michael Collins blasted off in the Apollo 11 spacecraft, on a mission watched by some 600 million people around the world.

On July 20, they landed safely on the Moon, after almost ending up in a rocky field where, Michael Collins remembers, "Some of these boulders were the size of Volkswagens!"

Neil Armstrong, the first man to set foot on the Moon's surface, described it as "beautiful," but Buzz Aldrin thought otherwise, calling it "desolate" and "totally lifeless," with little to see but "shades of gray and a black horizon." For many viewers watching at home, however, this was an awesome feat of near-magic, and the stuff of science fiction.

THE MOON

Long before Galileo looked up into the night sky with his telescope and realized its surface was rough and full of craters, mankind was fascinated by the lump of rock lighting up our night sky from more than 200,000 miles (320,000 km) away. Just think about the importance of the Moon in our myths and legends. Both Buddhist and Native American folklore, for example, tell of a rabbit who lives on the Moon, whereas some Inuit people believe the Moon to be a god named Anningan, who chases his sister Malina, the Sun goddess, across the sky. He's known to be forgetful when it comes to eating, which is why we see the Moon appear to grow thinner and thinner as the lunar cycle goes on, until he eventually reaches his crescent shape.

THE LUNAR CYCLE

The Moon goes through eight different phases every month.

1. NEW MOON
We can't actually see the Moon during this phase as the side that faces the Earth is not being lit by the Sun.

2. WAXING CRESCENT MOON
The Moon starts to show itself to us during this phase but only for a few minutes after sunset. Each day this visible period lasts a little longer.

3. FIRST QUARTER MOON
During this phase we will see half of the Moon for the first half of the evening, but it will disappear for the second half.

4. WAXING GIBBOUS MOON
Now we can see almost the entire Moon, for most of the night. As each night of this phase passes, we see a little bit more of the Moon.

8. WANING CRESCENT MOON
During this phase, a small slice of the Moon appears in the sky at the end of the night. As each day of the phase passes, the Moon can be seen for less time, until it disappears to become a New Moon again!

7. THIRD QUARTER MOON
During this phase we will see half of the Moon for the second half of the night.

6. WANING GIBBOUS MOON
We can see almost the entire Moon again, for most of the night, just like during the Waxing Gibbous phase, but now we see a little less of the Moon with every night that passes.

5. FULL MOON
Finally, we can see the entire Moon for the entire night.

MOON MADNESS

The Moon has always been associated with madness, although scientists have never found any real evidence to link the two. In the fifth century BC, the famous Ancient Greek doctor Hippocrates wrote that "one who is seized with terror, fright, and madness during the night is being visited by the goddess of the moon."

This idea has carried on throughout history. In England in the 18th century, you could seek a reduced sentence in a murder trial on the grounds of lunacy (madness) if your crime happened during a Full Moon. (The word "lunacy" comes from the Latin word *luna* or "moon.")

BY THE LIGHT OF THE MOON

During a Full Moon, eagle owls inflate their white throat feathers to catch the light when calling to each other, antlion larvae make bigger holes in the ground, and some sea turtles use the high tide to surf the waves up onto the shore and lay their eggs on the beach. Then there's the Moon-induced mass-spawning that takes place in the Great Barrier Reef in November to December each year, where hundreds of coral species spawn together in an awesome show of natural timing.

ARE ALL STARS CREATED EQUAL?

As well as the difference in brightness between stars, which comes from a combination of their closeness to Earth and their burning power, we might also see differences in color, which are due to the stars' different temperatures. Blue stars are the hottest, then come white stars like our Sun, and finally we have red stars, which are the coolest.

THE LIFE OF A STAR

Like humans, stars grow, change, and shrink over the course of their lives. Beginning as balls of gas and cold dust, they start to shine when their centers get hot enough to turn hydrogen to helium. This process is called nuclear fusion, and it creates a huge amount of energy, which is given off in light and heat by the stars.

The biggest stars burn for (only!) tens of millions of years before they run out of energy, whereas medium-sized stars like our Sun can keep burning for 10 billion years!

From where we stand on the ground, the stars above us often seem to twinkle, but this is actually Earth's stormy atmosphere at work. Out in space, the stars are perfectly still!

THE MILKY WAY

If we look up at the sky on a clear night, we can see about 3,000 stars. With binoculars or a telescope we can see many thousands more, and every last one of these is part of our own galaxy — the Milky Way, which has a staggering 200 billion stars or so altogether.

The size of the Milky Way is mind-blowing, but even more incredible is the fact that there are hundreds of billions of galaxies like ours in the universe.

With the help of the Earth-orbiting Hubble Space Telescope, launched in 1990, we've been able to map them out to a distance of 13 billion light years away!

WE ARE STARDUST

THE DEATH OF A STAR

In a way, stars are like huge ovens. Their fiery heat causes things to mix inside them to make something new. (Think of how a cake is made!)

Late in their lives, the biggest stars will explode and, when they do, they fling the materials they've formed far out into the universe. A massive 40,000 tons of this cosmic dust falls on Earth every year.

We generally can't see it, unless a chunk of it, called a meteorite, falls to Earth, but it gets into our soil, our plants, our animals, and eventually us. So we could have particles in us that are as old as the universe!

THE CELESTIAL SPHERE

The night sky looks a lot like a huge dome with stars attached to the inside surface. If we could look through the Earth, we'd see the other half of this starry dome, as if we were standing in the middle of a globe of stars. This is our celestial sphere. Some of its stars are so far away that it takes their light up to 2,000 years to reach our eyes. So when we're looking up at the night sky, some of the light we can see is already many centuries in the past!

THE NORTH STAR

The North Star (or Polaris) isn't actually the brightest star in the sky; that honor goes to Sirius, the Dog Star. It's just very noticeable in the northern hemisphere because it sits almost directly above the North Pole. There's no star like that at the South Pole now and there won't be for another 2,000 years, but eventually that may change, just as we will eventually get a new North Star (Gamma Cephei).

This is because of the way the Earth spins at a tilted angle, thanks to the gravitational tugging of the Sun and Moon. One complete spin takes 26,000 years, though, so Polaris will be with us as the North Star for a while yet!

The Paiute Native Americans traditionally thought of the stars as children of the Sun and Moon. This sounds sweet, until we learn that the reason stars can't be seen in the daytime is that their Sun father eats them every morning! Still, at least the stars are loved by their Moon mother,

Now we know the stars are not celestial children, or heavenly peepholes for the gods, or the eyes of our dead relatives as some have believed in the past. They are balls of fiery gas, tens of trillions of miles away. Even our closest star, Proxima Centauri, would take 78,000 years to reach

STARGAZING: LOOK UP!

CAMELOPARDALIS THE GIRAFFE

This faint constellation was first recorded in 1624. Its name comes from the Latin take on the Greek word for giraffe, which breaks down as "camel-leopard," because giraffes have long necks like camels and spotty skin like leopards.

BIG BEAR, LITTLE BEAR: URSA MAJOR AND URSA MINOR

Greek legend tells of a nymph named Callisto who had a baby named Arcas with Zeus, the king of the gods. This made Zeus's wife Hera so angry that she turned Callisto into a bear. Many years later, when Arcas almost killed this bear, Zeus transformed him into a bear, too, and threw them both into the sky.

Callisto became Ursa Major (the Great Bear and the northern sky's biggest constellation) and Arcas became Ursa Minor (the Little Bear). Hera was said to be so enraged by this that she banned the pair from bathing, which is why they never dip below the horizon!

CAMELOPARDALIS

CASSIOPEIA

THE NORTH STAR

CEPHEUS

URSA MAJOR

URSA MINOR

CASSIOPEIA THE QUEEN AND CEPHEUS THE KING

Cassiopeia was a vain Ethiopian queen from Greek mythology. When she bragged that she and her daughter Andromeda were more beautiful than the sea nymphs, the sea god Poseidon was furious, and sent the sea monster Cetus to destroy their kingdom. Just as Cassiopeia and her husband, Cepheus, were about to sacrifice poor Andromeda to Cetus to save the kingdom, heroic Perseus rode in on Pegasus (his famous winged horse) to rescue her.

Poseidon refused to let the royals go unpunished, and he turned Cassiopeia and Cepheus into constellations. Cassiopeia's extra punishment was to be tied to a chair facing the North Star. Because of this, she's forced to spend half the night hanging upside down!

DRACO THE DRAGON

There are all sorts of myths about how this constellation came to be. For example…

- Was Draco the dragon guard of the golden apples in the Garden of Hesperides? In this myth, the famous hero Hercules was challenged to steal the apples and, when he did so, he killed the dragon, which was sent to the heavens for defending this precious fruit to the death!

- Is Draco the dragon who attacked the goddess Athena? In this story she flung her attacker into the air, and his body stayed twisted in the heavens forever.

DRACO

The stars in our night sky have been arranged by poets, farmers, and astronomers over thousands of years into dot-to-dot-style pictures called constellations.

There are 88 official constellations across the whole of the night sky. Many come from the Ancient Greeks, and their names have their roots in Greek legends.

Because of the Earth's rotation around the Sun, not all constellations can be seen at all times of the year. Circumpolar constellations are the exception, because they sit above the North and South Poles.

Stargazers can see these constellations above the horizon all night and all year. Look up — can you find them all?

POLAR CONSTELLATIONS OF THE SOUTHERN HEMISPHERE

THE SOUTHERN CROSS OR CRUX
The smallest recognized constellation, the Southern Cross (or Crux) is one of the most famous shapes in the night sky. Its stars are found on the flags of Australia, Papua New Guinea, New Zealand, and Brazil; it is represented in stone at Machu Picchu in Peru; and the New Zealand Maori people know it as "Te Punga," or "the anchor."

CRUX

CARINA

CENTAURUS

CARINA
This constellation is named after the Latin word for the keel (or bottom) of a ship. It was originally part of a bigger constellation called the Argo Navis, which was named after the ship *Argo* that Ancient Greek legends Jason and the Argonauts used in their quest to find a golden fleece that would help Jason reclaim his throne from his wicked uncle.

MIDDLE EARTH
People living at the world's equator don't have circumpolar constellations visible all year round. Their stars all change from season to season!

CENTAURUS
This constellation, one of the biggest in the sky, is meant to represent the centaur (a half-man, half-horse creature that is popular in Ancient Greek myth). People disagree on which centaur it is up there, but most people believe it is Chiron, the immortal centaur and famous teacher of Greek heroes Hercules, Theseus, Peleus, Achilles, and Perseus, who was placed in the stars by Zeus as a mark of respect.

WONDERS OF THE NIGHT SKY

Our sky is filled with wonders every night of the week. The huge piece of rock we call the Moon, backlit as it is by a cosmic fireball, even controls our tides with its immense gravitational pull, while 200 billion or so glittering lights rotate in the blackness above us. But the night has even more magic up its sleeve. Let's take a look now at some of the more extraordinary events the night sky has to offer.

SHOOTING STARS
AND METEOR SHOWERS

If we peer up at the sky on a crystal-clear night for long enough, we should be able to see a shooting star. These are not real stars but meteoroids (little pieces of rock or dust that hit the Earth's atmosphere and begin to burn up). As they burn, they streak bright light across the night sky, creating the "shooting" effect.

To some Native American tribes, shooting stars were the traveling spirits of heroes; to others, they were omens of war or the poop of stars! In 2015, NASA reminded us that during his year in space, astronaut Scott Kelly would produce more than 175 pounds (80 kg) of poop that would be ejected into space and burn up in the atmosphere just like a shooting star!

Sometimes the Earth will get caught up in what's called a comet trail. Then we might see up to 100 shooting stars per hour as the amount of dust and rock burning up in the atmosphere soars. These meteor showers can light up the entire sky, as during the Leonid shower in 1966, when 40 shooting stars could be seen every second!

AURORAS

Every year, between November and April in countries close to the Arctic Circle (or between March and September in places close to Antarctica), we can watch the *aurora borealis* (northern lights) or the *aurora australis* (southern lights) filling the night sky with waves of bright blue, green, pink, and purple light. Visitors to dark-skied places from Svalbard to Scotland describe seeing these magical lights as one of the most amazing experiences of their lives.

So what causes these bright lights to dance through the darkness? Well, auroras (named after Aurora, the Roman goddess of the dawn) take place when the Sun spits out electrically charged particles that collide with atoms and molecules in the Earth's upper atmosphere, creating little bursts of light that together make up a much bigger flash. But many more magical explanations can be found in folklore....

To the Scandinavian Sami people, the northern lights were the souls of the dead, whereas Scots saw them as dancers and Finns saw them as the tails of Arctic foxes scurrying across the sky. To the Australian Gunai, the southern lights were bushfires in the spirit world, whereas the New Zealand Maori more cheerily imagined their ancestors having sky bonfires!

MOONBOWS

As if to show us that it can do everything the day can do, the night will sometimes present lucky sky-gazers with a moonbow, which is a rainbow created by moonlight instead of sunlight.

It works in exactly the same way as a rainbow: many tiny drops of water in rain or waterfalls separate the colors from a beam of light so they appear to us as bands of color (because of the way the light bends) when we look at them from a certain position.

Moonbows aren't as colorful as rainbows — they often look white to the naked eye — because moonlight is weaker than sunlight. But they have an eerie magic that is all their own.

THE
EARTH
AT NIGHT

"A man is a very small thing, and the night is very large and full of wonders."

— Edward Plunkett

When night falls on our corner of the Earth, most humans start thinking about getting some sleep, but by no means are all of the world's species diurnal (day-wakers) like us. For the majority of living creatures, when darkness falls and the Moon and stars come out, it's time to rise and shine and begin a brand-new day. Our deserts become cooler and more hospitable places for wildlife, our savannas become the playground of top predators, our rain forests become a riot of sound, and our mountains and cities are ruled by residents rarely seen in the daytime....

URBAN GLOW

In Hong Kong, the urban night sky can be a thousand times brighter than the international norm, and the sky glow of Los Angeles can be seen from 200 miles (320 km) away. We're not just lighting rooms — we're lighting the world itself. In an average year in the United States, enough outdoor lighting is used, mostly for streetlights and parking lots, to meet the energy needs of New York City for two years!

QUICK-FINGERED FORAGERS

Raccoons and opossums are masterful at keeping out of the way of humans, as well as finding food. They share an ability to eat and digest almost anything, and they have nifty "fingers" that help them to open containers like garbage cans, where they might find rich pickings of discarded food.

SPIKY SURVIVORS

In places like London, England, where empty city skyscrapers and shops leave their lights on all night and streetlights are numerous, some birds begin their dawn chorus in the early hours, confused by the light signals, while human sleepers take refuge behind blackout blinds and sleep masks. For many animals, city nightlife is problematic, but others have adapted remarkably well. One of these is the hedgehog, which can now be found in more urban areas than rural ones. When researchers at the University of Hamburg started tracking these prickly creatures, they found that while they mostly stuck to private yards in the daytime, at night they took over public parks to find food and mates.

IT'S ALL FOOD TO FOXES

Red foxes are a common feature of the urban night. Foxes are known to be clever; they adapt quickly to changing environments and, like raccoons and opossums, they can eat all kinds of food. Another crucial factor in their success as urban animals is that they have developed incredible immune systems (that's the part of your body that fights off illness), so they can quite literally eat any old garbage and thrive!

THE CITY

Humans have had an impact all over the world, bringing technology, settlements, noise, and light pollution to virtually every corner of the globe, but nowhere is our experience of the night more different from that of ancient humans than in our cities, which are so bright that their lights can be seen quite clearly from space.

The desert may be hot and harsh for the most part, but especially at night, life can be found here. And for the many people in the world living under murky urban skies, it may just offer a touch of celestial magic, too.

THE QUEEN OF THE NIGHT

Deserts may be short on vegetation, but the plants that do live here are amazing survivors. One of the most interesting is a particular species of night-blooming cereus, *Selenicereus grandiflorus*, also known as the Queen of the Night. A part of the cactus family, if we passed it in the day or on most nights of the year, we'd see nothing but a dry, dead-looking bush. But on one special night a year at midsummer, its beautiful and pleasant-smelling flowers open, before closing forever as the Sun comes up the next morning.

THE DESERT

Deserts are famously dry and inhospitable, and are generally the hottest places on Earth, with the exception of polar deserts. But some deserts that get as hot as 120°F (49°C) during the day drop to 0°F (-18°C) at night. When this happens, the many desert animals who have hidden as best they can during the day to conserve energy and avoid the scorching heat begin to walk the sands.

STARGAZING

Deserts are amazing destinations for intrepid stargazers looking to escape the light pollution in towns and cities. When the Sun sets on Africa's Namib Desert, the Milky Way unfolds overhead with almost impossible sharpness, and familiar constellations are surrounded by stars that can't even be seen from small towns. But even this place can't top Chile's Atacama Desert. It gets about 200 cloudless nights every year, and this combines with its high altitude and minimal light pollution to make it an incredible place to see the night skies. Scientists obviously agree, as it's the home of two world-class observatories.

BIG EARS

Many desert animals have adaptations that make them more suitable for nocturnal desert life. Fennec foxes, for example, have oversized ears that let out body heat and help with their excellent sense of hearing, which lets them find prey under the dark desert skies.

THE SANDS OF TIME

The southern Namib Desert (our world's oldest desert) looks like something from the planet Mars in the daytime, with its mountainous red sand dunes and a climate so harsh that 600-year-old dead trees can be found there. These odd landmarks have been burned black by the Sun but are unable to decompose because conditions are just too dry!

BURROWING

Like many other desert animals such as toads and mice, jerboa stay in their underground burrows during the day to avoid the worst of the heat. When they come out to hunt at night, their big eyes let them make the most of the low light, and their long whiskers help them feel their way around.

THE RAIN FOREST

Some places quiet down at night, but not the rain forest. As darkness falls, hundreds of cricket and katydid species begin to rub their wings together to make a screeching hum, joined by the shrill sounds of howler monkeys at dusk and dawn.

When the rainy season hits, things get louder still, as thousands of frogs come out to newly created ponds and streams to breed in shrieking fashion. Some tree frogs ramp up the noise level even further by using rolled-up leaves as loudspeakers for their calls.

But the prize for the greatest racket must go to the mighty bulldog bat, whose shrieks can hit an ear-splitting 140 decibels. That's 20 decibels louder than the average rock concert and 15 decibels louder than the average human pain threshold. Luckily the frequency of the bat's squeal is too high to be heard by human ears!

GLOWING

The rain forest at night is not as dark as we might expect. In the Amazon, for example, we might stumble on railroad worms, whose heads glow traffic-light red, while their bodies sport several pairs of glowing green spots.

We might pass fireflies flashing their rhythmic lights to attract mates, or even eerie green luminous fungus! Then there are the huge glowing eyes of tarsiers, scanning the landscape for frogs, insects, or lizards to snack on....

SOMEONE'S WATCHING YOU

Another interesting moon-eyed animal found clinging to the rain forest's trees at night is the aye-aye. These scruffy creatures are the only primates with echolocation skills, meaning that they use sound waves and echoes to figure out where things are. They find insect larvae to eat by tapping on tree trunks!

BLOODSUCKERS

Among the many bats that flap through the canopy of the rain forest at night, one is particularly famous: the vampire bat. Weighing in at only 1 pound (500 g), these strange-looking creatures have wide mouths and extremely sharp teeth.

Vampire bats drink about a teaspoon of blood from each victim so, despite their fearsome reputation, they can't really harm humans, except by spreading malaria. They are actually quite caring, sociable creatures, unique among bats for the way they share food with each other.

TRIBAL LIFE

The Amazon rain forest is home to many indigenous tribes. In fact, there are more uncontacted tribes spending their nights here than anywhere else in the world. Sadly, their way of life is being threatened by the destruction of the rain forest.

The Amazon's Awá people live in harmony with nature under the rain forest's thick canopy, hunting with large bows and arrows. They know the rain forest well, but they don't eat everything it provides. Large opossums, for example, are too smelly, and bats are thought to cause headaches when eaten.

THE MOUNTAINS

At night, the soaring, magical views of Earth's majestic mountains are reduced to an eerie blackness, their slopes are freezing cold, and their air is thin. Their dizzy heights make them unsuitable for all but the toughest humans, plants, and animals...and, if we believe the legends, the famous yeti. But there are consolations for the harsh climate. Remote ranges have little light pollution, and their high altitude gives night visitors a spectacular view of starry skies.

MOUNTAIN FLYER

The extreme-altitude night-flying of the bar-headed goose has long baffled scientists. These birds can fly at heights where only 10% of the oxygen found at sea level remains.

A New Zealand climber claimed to have seen them flying over the top of Mount Everest, which stands at 29,029 feet (8,848 m), and they have been tracked flying as high as 23,999 feet (7,315 m). Researchers believe they fly at night because the air is colder and denser.

MOUNTAIN CLIMBER

Humans have always been attracted to mountain ranges like the Himalayas, and especially to Mount Everest. But these are not easy places for humans to be, especially overnight. Climbers hoping to scale the famous peak can expect nights spent under freezing cold skies — even average summer temperatures on Everest are around -2°F (-19°C), and daytime temperatures drop more than 18°F (10°C) once darkness falls. These temperatures, combined with the thin air of the high altitude, make it difficult to sleep, think, and even breathe.

MOUNTAIN STALKER

Mountaintops are not just short on human life — their harsh conditions make it difficult for animals and plants to thrive, too, but a couple of animals do prowl the snowy ground at night, most notably the elusive snow leopard. These beautiful creatures are known as the ghosts of the mountains because so little is known about them. They may hunt in the daytime when they don't sense human presence, but mostly they are creatures of the night.

MOUNTAIN BEAUTY

The farther we go down a mountain, the more nocturnal life we will find. One particularly pretty resident of the Himalayan foothills who patrols the night is the red panda. These cute, cat-sized creatures, who look nothing like their black-and-white cousins, spend their days sleeping in high branches to avoid attackers, and only come down at night.

MOUNTAIN LEGEND

The existence of the yeti or "abominable snowman" has never been proven, but he is said by believers to be a huge, ape-like creature who stalks the dark, steep slopes of the Himalayas between the treeline and permanent snow.

Sherpa tradition says that he will only show himself to people who believe in him, so if you find yourself wandering in the Himalayas at night, keep your mind open and your eyes peeled....

THE SAVANNA

The iconic image of the savanna is of a hot, dry, dusty plain with hardy trees and majestic animals, but savannas actually have three seasons: hot and dry, cool and dry, and warm and wet. Their rainy season and cooler season make them more friendly to life than deserts, but their heat — even in the cool season, temperatures range from 68° to 78°F (20°–25°C) — means that many animals prefer to come out at night.

SNACK TIME

The mighty African elephant, who forages for a tiring 14 hours a day, may still be awake as night falls. Among the night-wandering animals of the savanna, elephants are perhaps the farmer's biggest nuisance, as they can eat around 660 pounds (300 kg) of food over 24 hours — that's enough to completely wipe out someone's crops over the course of one night!

When they're not fixating on food, elephants can be found during the dark hours forming a tight circle around their calves. The adults' immense size makes them troublesome prey for lions and leopards, but calves can easily be picked off under cover of darkness if they're not properly protected.

TRAVELERS AND DEFENDERS

It's not uncommon to see an aardvark trudging through the savanna night: these dogged termite-eaters have been found traveling 20 miles (30 km) a night in search of food.

Or we might, if we're lucky, spot an African civet guarding its patch — these elusive and solitary nocturnal animals mark their territory with a special scent that is also used in perfume and coffee. No two civets have the same fur patterns or markings. These beautiful night-dwellers are as individual as snowflakes!

SOUNDS OF THE SAVANNA

Visitors who prick up their ears in the savanna at night may hear the squeaks of yellow-winged bats as they test the air for tasty mosquitoes nearby, the scraping slither of rock pythons through the dust, or the deep-throated growls of aardwolves defending their territory.

NOISY NEIGHBORS

Hyenas are social animals who work hard together to find food, and they communicate with as many as 20 different calls. Their whooping, which is loud enough to echo more than several miles, calls other hyenas to food or a patch that needs defending. Their famous cackling is a sign of frustration at being chased or attacked by other hyenas.

IT'S DARK OUT THERE!

The lesser bushbaby is unusual among animals who are active at night. Despite its nocturnal habits, scientists have often wondered whether it's afraid of the dark, since it stays in a familiar tree when there's no moonlight, yet it travels far and wide when the Moon is there to light its way!

A FEARSOME WARRIOR

Honey badgers are basically shy animals but, when cornered, they come out fighting, with claws to rival bears, thick fur, tough skin, and a bite that can send even a lion running in the other direction. They love honey more than anything and are so resilient that they can even cope with attacks from swarms of bees. It's best not to get in their way!

ARMORED BUT UNDER ATTACK

Pangolins, with their otherworldly armor-plated bodies, have no teeth but an incredibly long tongue. At nearly 20 inches (50 cm) long, it is longer than their body when fully stretched out, and they use it to suck termites out of mounds, which they find with a strong sense of smell that is ideal for night-foraging.

When attacked, pangolins roll up into razor-sharp balls but, sadly, poachers still roam the darkness looking for them as their scales are highly valued. In fact, these beautiful creatures are the most trafficked animal in the world.

THE FOREST

As the last crow makes its way home to roost and a thick carpet of darkness falls on the trees, all sorts of rustling, howling, and squeaking begins in the forest. Bats unfurl their wings and head out to find food, foxes begin their prowl, and shy deer come out to graze. Badgers poke their heads up from their deep underground setts and venture out in search of breakfast, fresh bedding, and space to play.

Toads crawl out from under the large, cool stones or piles of damp, rotten wood they've been hiding under to avoid the daytime sunshine, which quickly dehydrates their dry, rough skin. Once up and about, male toads start up a croaking chorus, especially near ponds or other water. Their plan is to convince the female toads that their throaty song makes them the best match, and competition for mates is fierce.

PATHFINDERS

The wood mouse has an interesting way of navigating the land. These tiny nightcrawlers actually find their way around their territory by using clear place markers like leaves and twigs at important positions, so they know where they're going. They are the only creature, aside from humans, that are known to do this.

INTO THE NIGHT AIR

The majestic barn owl used to be thought of as a bad omen (a sudden screech at the window of a sick person was thought to be a sign that he or she would die), but these birds are now much-loved icons of the woods.

Those who get too close to a barn owl's nest or chicks might hear a loud, scary hiss. Single barn owls looking for a partner can also make quite a racket. Their mating season coincides with Halloween, making their nightly screaming even more eerie.

HUMANS OF THE WOODS

Green and delightful by day, the woods can be scary at night for humans not used to their sounds and moving shadows. But for fans of the wild life, like Emma Orbach, there is no greater place to make your home.

Despite having grown up in a Victorian castle, this Oxford University graduate now lives in a hut without electricity in an isolated corner of west Wales, United Kingdom, where she keeps goats and chickens, grows vegetables, and collects her water from streams. At night, she sleeps among the noises of the forest animals in a roundhouse made from mud, straw, and horse manure!

THE SHIMMERING SHORE

The sea at night is not all darkness and gloom. One of its brightest and most fascinating nighttime features is the phenomenon of bioluminescent plankton, also known as sea sparkle, which produces an electric bright blue glow at night whenever it is disturbed.

Bioluminescent plankton are so small that one drop of bright blue water has thousands swimming in it! The plankton's colorful flashing is thought to be a defense mechanism against predators, since bright colors in nature often indicate a toxic animal.

A LIVING FLOOR

When night falls, zooplankton journey up from deep waters to nearer the ocean's surface. Moving together in a huge horde, these tiny creatures create an effect that is something like a living snowstorm. They form such a solid layer that submarines have been able to hide under it undetected, with sonar readings taking the living carpet of plankton to be the seabed!

This nightly influx of plankton affects the waters around it massively, as a variety of fish, and even dolphins and sharks, follow their food closer to the water's surface. So although the ocean may look dark and still at night, there's an amazing amount of activity just below the surface, with many creatures just now stirring to life.

THE OCEAN

The ocean at night is dark and still rather mysterious to humans, but there are some fascinating things going on beneath its black surface. Take hard coral, for instance — if we look at it in the daytime, it appears to be completely static, even dead, but at night, its soft tentacles wave into the water in an effort to collect tiny zooplankton to eat. Of course, coral is not the only ocean creature to wake up when the Sun sets....

SQUID SECRETS

The giant squid is a truly fascinating being. These enormous and elusive creatures have the biggest eyes of any animal, at a huge 10 inches (25 cm) wide! These powerful peepers allow them to spot a meal in the dark waters where most creatures wouldn't be able to see. Giant squid are still very mysterious to us, as the deep water they live in is difficult to get to and study.

THE DARKEST OF DEPTHS

In the deepest sea, it is permanently night, and the creatures that live in these cold, sunless places have adapted to it quite spectacularly. The female anglerfish, for example, has a kind of long pole above her head with a light at the end of it, which attracts prey that she then chomps in her sharp, translucent teeth.

NIGHT SWIMMERS

Lobsters who hide in cozy corners of coral reefs during the daytime emerge at night to find food, as does the creepy-looking moray eel. This night swimmer has terrible eyesight but a fantastic sense of smell, which makes it well adapted to hunting in the dark ocean waters.

MASTERS OF DISGUISE

Another interesting sea creature we're most likely to see once darkness falls is the octopus. These shy sea-dwellers are built to hide from, rather than fight, attackers, and they stay in their dens during the day, only going out to hunt for food under the cover of darkness.

With no internal skeleton, octopuses can change shape in amazing ways, and many can change color to match their environment, making them tough for predators to spot.

ANIMALS
AT NIGHT

"The day has eyes; the night has ears."

— David Fergusson

Animals' night lives are a mystery to most of us. Can birds sleep in the air? Do marine animals sleep while swimming? Do cats and dogs dream like we do? While we humans are sleeping, the world's nocturnal animals are out and about, but just how have they adapted to life in the dark landscape of the night? How do their senses differ from ours?; how do they see so well in the dark?; and what tricks do they use when it comes to finding food?

STANDING SLEEPERS

Despite only sleeping for around half an hour a day, the giraffe doesn't doze in a single shift — in fact, it naps for bursts of a few minutes at a time, hoping that this will be safer. Another adaptation that protects giraffes, as well as horses, zebras, flamingos, and elephants, is something called "stay apparatus," a locking mechanism that allows them to sleep standing up, so they can run away on short notice if necessary. The Guinea baboon has a similar strategy. It sleeps on its heels at the top of a tree, where it can spring into action as soon as either predator or prey approaches.

SLEEP AND DREAMS

All living creatures need sleep to survive. Meat-eating animals tend to get more time asleep than plant-eating animals, as the plant-eaters usually spend a lot of time watching out for meat-eaters who may want to snack on them! A good comparison is the giraffe, who sleeps for around half an hour a day on average, and the lion, who snoozes for more than 15 hours a day!

Even the mighty lion, though, is no match for the desert snail. This slow-moving creature can sleep for years on end when it senses that conditions aren't right for active living. In 1850, a desert snail being exhibited in the British Museum had been glued to a card for four years before it was found to be alive, and was revived!

SAFE SLEEPERS

Sleep safety is hugely important to wild animals, as predators are always lurking. Because of this, ducks like to sleep in rows with two lookout guards at either end, while meerkats sleep in a big pile, with the leader buried in the safest spot at the bottom.

Huddling up for warmth during sleep is not just something practiced among meerkats — squirrels, puppies, bats, and others are known to do the same thing.

SOARING SLEEPERS

Amazingly, some creatures can even sleep on the move! While most birds sleep in trees, the mighty albatross, who is said to be able to fly 10,000 miles (16,000 km) just to deliver food to its chick, is able to sleep while flying, as is Swainson's thrush, which also flies long distances. These birds take hundreds of little power naps a day, and each lasts only a few seconds, which hardly seems very refreshing, but it seems to work for them!

SOPHISTICATED SLEEPERS

So how do our closest animal relatives sleep? Well, orangutans, chimps, and gorillas tend to sleep quite a lot, like us. They find platforms to build beds on so they can sleep for longer without being attacked by predators, and their nest-building process is very complicated. Orangutans start learning to build nests at six months old (the skills take a few years to master) and as part of their training, they even learn how to weave branches and leaves together to make mattresses!

Apes curl up to sleep just like we do, and they're also pretty fussy about which trees they make their nests in. In a study on a wildlife reserve in Uganda, nearly 75% of chimp nests were made in strong Ugandan ironwood trees, despite the fact that these made up less than 10% of the area's trees.

SWEET SLEEPERS

Many sea creatures have their own unique sleeping styles — like sea otters, who drape themselves in seaweed to stay anchored. These adorable animals can be found sleeping in groups called rafts of up to 100 otters, and individuals within a raft may even hold hands to keep themselves even more secure.

BLUBBER JACKETS

Walruses can sleep while swimming thanks to their pharyngeal pouches (neck air-pockets), which work like built-in life jackets! This impressive adaptation allows them to swim for more than 80 hours nonstop, and they can be seen bobbing in the ocean with just their nose and tusks visible.

SLEEPING WITH ONE EYE OPEN

Dolphins can go about their business for 15 days without stopping because they can literally sleep with one eye open. Half of their brain sleeps at a time, while the other half carries on as normal.

They also have another, deeper kind of sleep called logging. During it, they float like logs on the surface of the water. Female dolphins don't get this kind of rest when they have newborn calves in tow, however. Calves swim along in their mother's slipstream, and their lack of body fat means they would sink without her help.

SINKING SLEEPERS

When hippos sleep in water, their bodies automatically bob up to the surface every few minutes so they can take a breath. So why don't these animals, who actually can't even swim, just sleep on land? The answer: it's a matter of moisture. If hippo skin dries out, it will crack uncomfortably, so these big beasts don't stray far from the watering hole.

DO ANIMALS DREAM LIKE WE DO?

Almost all mammals and birds (but not cold-blooded animals) go through the stage of REM (rapid eye movement) sleep that, in humans, is the dreaming stage. Researchers looking at the brain activity of sleeping rats discovered the same patterns happening at night as happened during the day when the rats were learning to make their way through a maze.

Were these rats dreaming about their daily activities like humans do? We don't know, but dogs sometimes seem to be chasing things in their sleep, and cats occasionally raise their heads and arch their backs as if they're stalking mice while they sleep. Even the platypus has been known to move in the same way during sleep as it would when hunting crustaceans while awake!

NOCTURNAL
ANIMALS

Unlike humans, some animals are designed to be active at night.
So what characteristics do these animals have in common that
make them suitable for life in the dark?

GLOWING

A bioluminescent animal is one that's capable of making its
own light. It might do this to communicate with others —
the deep-sea lantern fish uses bioluminescence to send
signals to its fellow fish in the dark waters — or to lure
prey, as is the case with the scary-looking anglerfish.

Another reason for bioluminescence is to find a mate. Female
fireflies, for example, are known to choose males with a higher
rate and strength of flash over other fireflies. Finally, an animal
may use bioluminescence to defend itself — like the ostracod,
which gives out a burst of light when it is swallowed that
hopefully makes its startled attacker spit it out.

HEARING

In the dark, hearing is very important when
it comes to survival. There are two common
hearing adaptations found in nocturnal animals.
One is asymmetrical hearing, which lets an
animal use both ears separately to figure out
where a sound is coming from. This can be
seen in great gray owls, who can hear rodents
moving under 2 feet (0.5 m) of snow! Many
nocturnal animals, including different kinds of
cats, also have cup-shaped ears, which make
sounds seem louder.

SEEING

While some aquatic creatures living in the water's darkest depths have evolved to be sightless (like the blind Mexican cave fish), many animals have responded to their dark worlds by developing eyesight that's better suited to it.

WIDE EYES

One very common nocturnal sight adaptation is big eyes with wide pupils that are designed to collect more light. The tarsier, for example, has huge eyes — if a human's eyes were as large in proportion to his or her body, they would be grapefruit-sized!

BLACK-AND-WHITE EYES

Nocturnal eyes are full of rod cells because these sense light, while cone cells sense color. Hedgehogs have only rod cells, making their vision black-and-white. In a low-light world, light is much more important than color for seeing something lurking in those rustling bushes!

BRIGHT EYES

Some nocturnal animals have eyes with a *tapetum lucidum* or "bright carpet." This carpet of cells in the eye works like a mirror that reflects even more light to the rod cells so the animal can see better. This is what gives animal eyes that eerie, glow-in-the-dark look.

DARK POWERS

There are a variety of other, more unusual, ways nocturnal animals make their world work for them. For example, raccoons' fingers are amazingly sensitive, which lets them find crayfish in the water at night. Lions' eyes are designed with white under-eye strips that can pick up and make the most of faint moonlight to enhance vision. Pythons have heat sensors in their top lips that can zero in on their warm-blooded prey. And vampire bats take echolocation to a whole new level. These famous blood-drinkers can tell people apart just by the way they breathe!

SMELLING

A good sense of smell is another useful feature in dark environments. Rats have an amazing sense of smell to go with their nocturnal habits. They even have a second smell organ (the vomeronasal organ), which can detect chemical signals! And a moth can sniff out a mate from more than 6 miles (10 km) away.

HUMANS
AT NIGHT

*"It is a common experience that a problem difficult at night is
resolved in the morning after the committee of sleep has worked on it."*

— John Steinbeck

For most humans, nighttime means sleep, or perhaps difficulty sleeping, whether it's in
a bed, in a hammock, or on a futon. It may be a time to meet the Sandman or another
night visitor bringing sweet dreams or maybe nightmares. At certain times of the year,
in places all over the world, the night erupts with human celebrations, fireworks, and
bonfires. And then, of course, there are places at the far ends of the globe where the
Sun doesn't set for half the year, while for the other half of the year, residents experience
night all day long....

RHYTHM OF THE NIGHT

All living creatures, from humans to plankton, have a kind of body clock, which drives how they move through their days and nights. Although modern industrial living, with light available throughout the night, means that we humans could easily stay up all night now if we wanted to, anyone who tries this will soon learn that nature has its own ways of pushing us back into our natural rhythm.

6:45 A.M.
Sharpest rise in blood pressure

7:30 A.M.
Melatonin secretion stops

9:00 A.M.
Highest testosterone secretion in males

10:00 A.M.
High alertness

2:30 P.M.
Best coordination

3:30 P.M.
Fastest reaction time

5:00 P.M.
Greatest heart efficiency

6:30 P.M.
Highest blood pressure

7:00 P.M.
Highest body temperature

9:00 P.M.
Melatonin secretion starts

2:00 A.M.
Deepest sleep

4:30 A.M.
Lowest body temperature

THE MASTER CLOCK
This "master clock" (the suprachiasmatic nucleus) in our brains controls the production of a hormone called melatonin, which makes us sleepy. It sits just above our optic nerves, which carry signals from our eyes to our brains. The master clock uses this information to manage our days. When there is less light coming into our eyes, it thinks it is nighttime and orders more melatonin. That's why we yawn at the movies!

IT'S ALL ABOUT CHEMISTRY
Our bodies take about a day to complete a full cycle where serotonin (a chemical that manages anxiety, happiness, and mood and is produced partly by contact with sunlight) converts to melatonin (the sleep chemical).

THE LUNAR CYCLE

We think of our body clocks as running on a 24-hour cycle like our days, but they actually run on a 25-hour cycle that's almost identical to the Moon's.

Like the lunar cycle, the human cycle has high and low "tides," or peaks and troughs of energy. Maybe you've noticed that after a post-lunch slump, you start to perk up at around 4 p.m.? The Spanish siesta (an afternoon rest or sleep) takes this body engineering into account!

Humans aren't the only creatures to run on cycles that match the Moon. Sooty terns seem at first to be breeding at random times in the year, when they're actually breeding within a day or two of every tenth full moon.

SLEEP CYCLE

An average night's sleep, 7 to 8 hours, is divided into five stages that are repeated a few times during sleep. Here's how they break down:

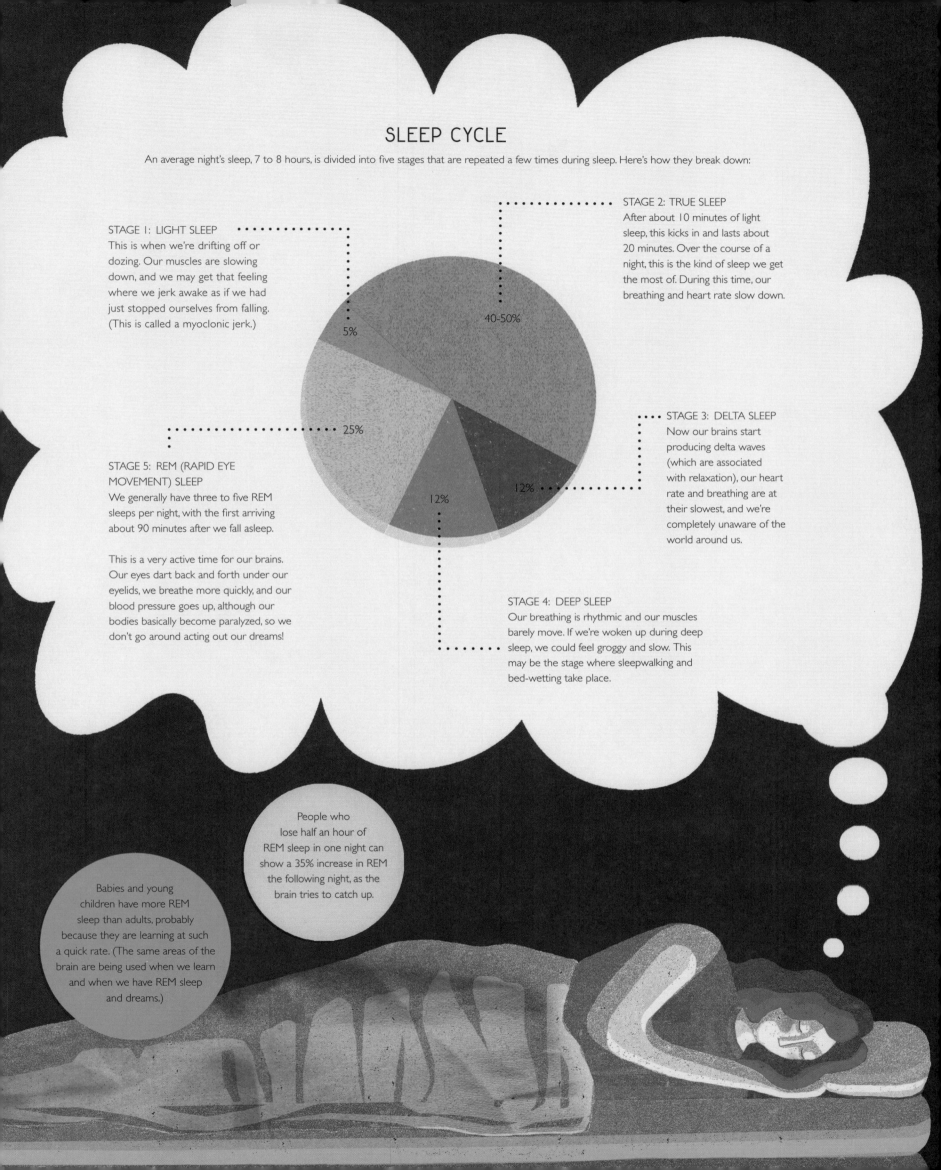

STAGE 1: LIGHT SLEEP
This is when we're drifting off or dozing. Our muscles are slowing down, and we may get that feeling where we jerk awake as if we had just stopped ourselves from falling. (This is called a myoclonic jerk.)

STAGE 2: TRUE SLEEP
After about 10 minutes of light sleep, this kicks in and lasts about 20 minutes. Over the course of a night, this is the kind of sleep we get the most of. During this time, our breathing and heart rate slow down.

STAGE 3: DELTA SLEEP
Now our brains start producing delta waves (which are associated with relaxation), our heart rate and breathing are at their slowest, and we're completely unaware of the world around us.

STAGE 5: REM (RAPID EYE MOVEMENT) SLEEP
We generally have three to five REM sleeps per night, with the first arriving about 90 minutes after we fall asleep.

This is a very active time for our brains. Our eyes dart back and forth under our eyelids, we breathe more quickly, and our blood pressure goes up, although our bodies basically become paralyzed, so we don't go around acting out our dreams!

STAGE 4: DEEP SLEEP
Our breathing is rhythmic and our muscles barely move. If we're woken up during deep sleep, we could feel groggy and slow. This may be the stage where sleepwalking and bed-wetting take place.

5%

40-50%

25%

12%

12%

People who lose half an hour of REM sleep in one night can show a 35% increase in REM the following night, as the brain tries to catch up.

Babies and young children have more REM sleep than adults, probably because they are learning at such a quick rate. (The same areas of the brain are being used when we learn and when we have REM sleep and dreams.)

Recent research has also suggested that we may have "hidden caves" in the brain that open up when we sleep. These are thought to help flush out brain toxins that are associated with diseases like Alzheimer's.

Our brains make connections (called synapses) when we do things and store memories. They get stronger as we practice skills and repeat actions. Scientists think these connections grow so frantically during the day that our brains can get overloaded but, when we sleep, they sort through and prune the connections, so we have what we need for the future.

The REM (rapid eye movement) stage of sleep, when we dream, is particularly useful for our memory of how to do things, and for processing emotional information, which may be why people often say that dreams are the body's way of sorting out our feelings and experiences from the day before.

REFRESHMENT FOR THE BRAIN

Sleep doesn't just rest our bodies, leaving us physically refreshed and ready to start a new day. It's also crucial when it comes to proper memory function, and it's key to helping us learn new things.

WHAT SLEEP MEANS TO US

Sleep is a big part of our lives. It's as important to our survival as eating and breathing, and we do an awful lot of it. In fact, the average person spends about a third of his or her life snoozing.

It's strange that we all end each day with a long period of unconsciousness, especially as this would traditionally leave us vulnerable to animal attacks...and yet, we have all evolved to continue doing it. Why? Scientists still don't entirely know. What we do know is that sleep gives our bodies a physical and mental break from daily activity, and this helps us to cope in different ways.

I CAN'T SLEEP!

We know that sleep is very important, but what happens to people when they don't get enough of it? Let's take a look.

UP ALL NIGHT

The world record for the longest time anyone has gone without sleep belongs to Randy Gardner. In 1965, he stayed awake for 11 days. During this time he started to hallucinate and have delusions that he was a famous soccer player! Guinness World Records has since stopped keeping records for staying awake as it could be dangerous.

EYES WIDE OPEN

FFI (Fatal Familial Insomnia) is a rare genetic disease that stops sufferers from sleeping for days on end. After a few weeks, they essentially start sleepwalking while awake and jerking the way we sometimes do when we're falling asleep.

Though most people's sleep loss is nowhere near as drastic as this, about a third of people will experience insomnia (difficulty sleeping) at some point in their lives. Various things contribute to this, like stress, noise, uncomfortable conditions, jet lag, night work, or medication. Foods that contain a chemical called tyramine, like bacon, cheese, and nuts, can also stop us from sleeping.

BY THE GLOW OF THE SCREEN

Another thing that can affect sleep is the blue light that comes from mobile phone and computer screens. It affects melatonin production, which then affects our sleep. Experts recommend avoiding these kinds of devices for at least an hour before we go to bed to avoid sleep disruption.

On the other hand, blue light can be useful for boosting attention levels and reaction times, and neuroscientists suggest that blue light exposure may be a useful tool for night workers or people with jet lag who want to get their body clocks into a certain rhythm.

SUPER SLEEPERS

We know sleep is crucial to humans, but are we all in the same boat when it comes to snoozing? In fact, 1–5% of the population are what scientists call "super-sleepers." This means they have a quirk in their DEC2 gene that allows them to get by on four to six hours of sleep a night and still feel totally fine the next day. Too much sleep (the seven or eight hours most of us need) leaves them feeling bleary and grumpy!

SANTA CLAUS

This jolly, red-suited fellow brings gifts to children all over the world on the night of December 24. Having traveled from his home at the North Pole with its workshop of elves, he rides a reindeer-drawn sleigh across the sky and climbs down the chimneys of homes to deliver wrapped presents. Apparently, he delivers presents to Australian children with the help of kangaroos rather than reindeer, though, and he visits Dutch kids via steamboat from Spain rather than traveling from the North Pole!

THE SANDMAN

The legendary sleep-bringer visits children in bed at night and sprinkles sleep dust in their eyes to send them off to the Land of Nod. The crust we call "sleep" that gathers in the corners of our eyes in the morning is proof of the Sandman's work.

But not all tales of the Sandman are quite so cheerful. In the 19th century, German author E.T.A. Hoffmann described him as "a wicked man who comes to children when they won't go to bed and throws a handful of sand into their eyes...he puts their eyes in a bag and carries them to the moon to feed his own children, who sit in the nest up there. They have crooked beaks like owls and can pick up the eyes of naughty human children." You have been warned!

THE TOOTH FAIRY

This generous sprite visits kids who have lost a baby tooth and leaves them a small gift, usually money, when they put the tooth under their pillow at night. But not everyone in the world offers their teeth up to the tooth fairy....

In many places, from Russia to New Zealand, some parents "sacrifice" the tooth to a "tooth rat" or "tooth mouse." This is supposed to ensure that the child's adult teeth will grow as strong and sturdy as a rodent's, whose teeth continue to grow throughout their lives!

DREAMS AND NIGHT VISITORS

During REM sleep, all humans dream, and the average person has about four dreams a night. Dreaming has always fascinated our species. As far back as Ancient Mesopotamia in 5000 BC, we have recorded our dreams. These days, we tend to see dreams as being about our feelings and experiences, whereas in the past, people often believed that dreams were otherworldly and could predict the future.

The Ancient Chinese, for example, believed that our Hun (or spiritual) soul could leave the body during sleep to commune with the gods and dead ancestors, while the Po (or physical) soul stayed in the body. The Ancient Greeks even had a dream-world god named Morpheus. He was the son of Hypnos (the god of sleep), and his job was to deliver the gods' messages to humans through their dreams. But he is not the only character to visit sleeping people at night. Let's take a look at some of the others.

NIGHTMARES

Scientists have found that the less REM sleep we get, the more intense our dreams become. Studies also show that "night owls," who prefer late nights to early mornings, have more frequent nightmares than "morning larks," who are most active at the beginning of the day. Research shows that women have around 15% more nightmares than men, and their frequency climbs during adolescence, peaks in young adulthood, and then drops as life goes on.

As for why we have nightmares at all, researchers think they may be the brain's way of trying to focus our attention on things that need addressing. Of course it may just be that every up has a corresponding down. After all, the Ancient Greek dream messenger, Morpheus, had a brother, Phobetor, who brought nightmares to people instead of dreams.

BAKU
This spirit animal from Japanese legend is known to helpfully eat the nightmares of sleeping people. Unfortunately, he sometimes gobbles up the person's hopes and ambitions at the same time, so a visit from him isn't always the answer to our bad dreams!

THE HISTORY OF HUMAN SLEEP

How did our ancestors sleep, and what would "natural" sleep look like to them? These days, we're told to try to get eight hours of unbroken sleep at night, during darkness hours. But has this always been the case across human history? Well, we don't have a time machine, but scientists have taken a look at non-industrial societies in Tanzania (the Hadza people), Bolivia (the Tsimane people), and Namibia (the San people) to try to get an idea of our natural sleep habits. These communities generally go to sleep around three and a half hours after the Sun sets and wake up before sunrise. They sleep through the night and take no daytime naps; generally they sleep outside or in huts. Interestingly, none of their languages has a word for insomnia.

LIGHT LIFE

Although volcanic gas vents were used in Beijing as early as 500 BC to help light the streets, it was not until 1667 that Paris introduced a system of public streetlights, which at that time were glass lamps with candles in them. Other cities then followed suit. By around 1745, more efficient oil lamps came about. Streetlights had started changing the night's landscape, as had lighting in homes and the opening of all-night coffee houses. Now night wasn't just a time when criminals could get away with crimes under cover of darkness — it was a time when respectable people could be active and socialize.

A SLEEP OF TWO HALVES

We haven't always slept in a single overnight chunk as we generally do now. Historian Roger Ekirch has found that, at least from around 1400, many Western people slept in two halves overnight, starting from a couple of hours after sunset, and with a break of a couple of hours in between the two stages, where they got up and even socialized.

During the Reformation (1517–1648), different religious groups started holding secret late-night services, which made the night seem more respectable. People who could afford to burn candles could also be active at night, which made it a newly fashionable time of day.

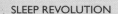

SLEEP REVOLUTION

As the Industrial Revolution (1760–1840) took hold and people started working longer hours to more rigid schedules, the two-sleep night became less and less popular. Toward the end of the 19ᵗʰ century, it started to be thought of as an inefficient and self-indulgent way to sleep. A single sleep was apparently better if you wanted to avoid headaches and constipation — and so our modern Western way of sleeping was born or, if we look at the research in Africa and Bolivia, we might say it was reborn!

RISE OF THE NIGHT OWLS

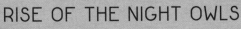

Although the Western world generally now opts for a single overnight sleep — this is not the case all over the world, as we will see — there are people, especially in big cities, bucking this trend. TV and the internet provide entertainment all night long, night owls who are able to set their own working hours may sleep during the day and come out at night, and on city streets we can see people coming out of 24-hour cafés, nightclubs, or simply coming and going.

And of course, there are the people keeping this nighttime economy afloat. Pastry chefs and bakers often work late-night shifts to make sure food is fresh

and ready for early-morning customers; hospital staff work night shifts since people get ill at all times of the day and night; security guards keep buildings safe during the dark hours; air traffic controllers head to their towers to manage night flights; and taxi drivers take night-owl passengers safely to their destinations.

It's a struggle for any human's body clock to adapt, and research suggests that we never truly get used to it, but just as humans have managed to make their homes in some of the most inhospitable corners of the world, so we have made inroads into the world of the night.

DARKNESS IN THE VILLAGE OF FLYING DOGS

While the southern hemisphere's extremes of day and night can only be seen in lonely Antarctica, the Arctic's can be experienced in countries like Iceland, Sweden, Russia, Finland, and Canada. So to look at the way this affects humans, let's observe Russia's remote Kola Peninsula, where for two months a year, residents go about their daily lives in darkness.

We could argue that humans were never meant to live in places where winter temperatures hit -40°F (-40°C) and Arctic winds roar relentlessly, causing the Peninsula's village of Gremikha to be known as the "village of flying dogs," since even a sled can be carried off by the gales there!

Certainly doctors now recognize that "polar night stress" is a real condition, but Kola doctor Lev Sokol believes that there is more to it than darkness. "The isolation factor here is very influential," he says. "There are no pleasant signs of nature around us, and the extreme temperatures and the winds affect people as much as the dark."

EXTREME DAY AND NIGHT

We know we need to get as much sleep as possible during the hours of darkness provided by nature, but these hours change with the seasons. For example, on the shortest day of the year in December in the UK in 2017, there were just under eight hours of sunlight, while on the longest day of the year in June, there were more than 16 hours of sunlight. This change happens because of the UK's position at around 55 degrees north of the equator, and the tilt of the Earth's axis. At the equator, the Sun rises and sets at the same time every day throughout the year, whereas near the Arctic and Antarctic Circles, the difference in daylight and darkness hours over the course of the year is extreme.

POLAR NIGHTS AND
THE MIDNIGHT SUN

In June, north of the Arctic Circle, we see the phenomenon of "midnight Sun," when the Sun doesn't set over the entire 24-hour cycle. In the Antarctic Circle, midnight Sun happens in December. The opposite of this is the "polar night," when the Sun doesn't rise over 24 hours. Polar night happens in the Arctic in December and in the Antarctic in June.

In places close to the poles, the Sun doesn't rise at all for half the year, and doesn't set for the other half of the year. This makes them pretty extreme environments for humans who are geared to sleep and wake with the coming and going of night's darkness.

SUNSET TO BLACKOUT:
THE POLAR NIGHT SPECTRUM

In Tromsø in Norway, which is more than 185 miles (300 km) north of the Arctic Circle, the polar night and midnight Sun each last for three months of the year — yet residents experience less winter depression than we might expect at this high latitude. This might be partly due to the huge number of festivals and celebrations the city holds during the winter, the opportunities to ski to work, the magnificent views of the northern lights, and the variety of efforts to make winter life something "koselig," or cozy, with its own special seasonal delights.

Another reason for residents' cheerfulness is probably that polar night in Tromsø is not a complete blackout. In the longer "days" at either end of the polar night season, residents are treated to sunrise and sunset colors in the sky for up to six hours, which is not the case on the Kola Peninsula. If we go as far north as Svalbard, Norway's most remote group of islands, there is no light change at all between day and night during the polar night season. Only 620 miles (1,000 km) or so from the North Pole, this isolated region can get as cold as -4°F (-20°C).

HOW THINGS GROW

Humans aren't the only life affected by the polar night and midnight Sun. Parts of Alaska, like the Tanana and Matanuska Valleys, are famous for their enormous vegetables, thanks to long hours of sunlight and warmth during the midnight Sun period — think 130-pound (60-kg) cabbages and even a single carrot that weighs more than 18 pounds (8 kg)!

So does the reversal of conditions created by the polar night hold things back in the other half of the year? Some studies have shown that it doesn't. Researchers measured the annual growth of white spruce trees in Alaska and Massachusetts and found that both trees produced the same amount of wood — the Alaskan trees just had that growth concentrated in their midnight Sun season, whereas the Massachusetts trees spread their growth throughout the year.

For animals, the long daylight hours of midnight Sun mean more chance for insects to breed and so more food for hungry birds. They also mean more feeding time for animals who find their food by catching sight of it, like caribou, who fatten themselves up enough during the summer to survive the harsh, dark winters that follow.

As far as the ocean goes, scientists no longer see the polar night as a time of icy stillness — in fact, it can be a dream for researchers, as the sea life that was lurking in deep waters is now swimming near the surface. Krill and plankton are even found feeding and reproducing during the polar night, as their body clocks seem not to change, perhaps because they are more sensitive to low levels of light than humans, so they can keep things more easily on track.

LIGHTING THE WAY

In 1933, American Bob Switzer was ordered by doctors to spend time in a darkened room to recover from a serious accident. While down in his basement, he and his magician brother Joe invented the world's first fluorescent paint. Bob painted his wife's wedding dress with it, creating the world's first piece of high-visibility clothing! Hi-vis is now worn all around the world by people who want to be seen in the dark.

SNAP AND GO

In the 1960s, scientists were hard at work trying to recreate the glow given off by fireflies and, by the 1970s, the glow stick was born. Though these became popular in the 1980s as party accessories at all-night dances, these colorful sticks also have more serious uses. Because they use cold light and don't produce potentially dangerous sparks or flames, they are a great choice for emergency lighting after natural disasters and mine exploration, and are also used in military kits all around the world.

STREETS AGLOW

In 2016, Mexican scientist José Carlos Rubio Avalos invented a cement that will allow buildings to glow in the dark for more than 100 years! The cement will glow even after cloudy days, and will work indoors as long as daylight comes in through the building's windows during the day. So far, available color choices are electric blue and bright green, but he's working on white, red, and purple glow-in-the-dark cement for the future.

SLEEP AROUND THE WORLD

All humans sleep, but not all cultures approach sleep in the same way. So how do our sleeping habits vary around the world?

A 2009 study showed that the French sleep for an average of almost nine hours a night. That's quite luxurious by world standards!

A 2013 Gallup poll showed that people in the U.S. only sleep for an average of 6.8 hours a night.

In Mexico, Spain, and other Mediterranean and Hispanic countries, a siesta (or daytime nap) for a few hours around lunchtime is traditional. The idea is to avoid the drowsiness of the post-lunch slump and to sleep through the hottest hours of the day. People can then return to work or study re-energized at around 4 p.m., which, if you look at the body clock diagram earlier in the book, works out quite nicely.

Modern hunter-gatherer tribes, such as the !Kung of the Kalahari desert, sleep whenever they're tired, whether it's day or night, light or dark.

In Scandinavia, fresh air is considered to be an important ingredient of a good nap, which is why we see rows of strollers outside cafés and shops in places like Norway and Sweden, even in the snowy winter! The belief that the fresh air will strengthen a child's immune system has even led to Scandinavian nurseries holding al fresco naptimes for infants!

A poll by the National Youth Policy Institute in hardworking South Korea saw Korean students sleeping for only 5 hours and 27 minutes a night on average!

Egyptians take a middle-of-the-day nap called a Ta'assila, which is much like a siesta.

The Temiars of Malaysia go for multiple sleeps over the course of 24 hours, with 25% of their people awake and active at any point of the day and night.

The Japanese have a practice of napping at the office called "inemuri," which translates as: "to be asleep while present." This is considered a mark of hard work, the idea being that you've worked yourself to the point of exhaustion. In order to give the correct impression, you should stay sitting up — conking out with your head on your desk is not good inemuri etiquette!

GETTING A GOOD NIGHT'S SLEEP

How we sleep has changed a lot over time, and varies considerably across different cultures. In Ancient Egypt, people feared sleep as the cousin of death and used stone pillows at night. Hard block pillows were also popular in ancient Asia, as soft pillows were thought to steal your energy (or "chi") while you slept. Japanese geishas had to use hard neck pillows to protect their elaborate hairstyles, and house mothers would spread sticky rice around the pillows to catch any geisha who let her head slip while she slept!

The Romans seem to have seen sleep as a kind of tedious distraction from empire-building, and despite their luxurious architecture, they tended to keep quite small, plain *cubicula* (rooms) for sleeping purposes.

In the Middle Ages, people tended to huddle together in communal beds, which kept in heat but also spread disease. During this time, pillows were seen as a sign of weakness and, in the 16th century, King Henry VIII of England banned everyone except pregnant women from using them!

LUXURIOUS SLEEPING

The Renaissance in Europe changed sleeping in a big way. Rigging was created for bed frames, and beds generally became more sophisticated and ornate, although soft pillows still didn't become popular until the Industrial Revolution. During this period in China, under the Ming dynasty, beds also became more beautiful, with big frames and pretty details on the wood.

SLEEPING STYLES

These days, most Western people sleep on sprung mattresses with soft pillows and a comforter, but this is not the case all over the world. For example, the !Kung people of the Kalahari often sleep on animal skins or just on the ground itself, while the Venezuelan Hiwi people sleep in hammocks, which are hugely popular across Latin America. Neither culture uses pillows or blankets, possibly because they can lead to more contact with fleas and lice. In areas where malaria is a problem, like Ethiopia and Mozambique, netted beds are common.

The traditional Japanese futon bed, which can be rolled up during the day, is popular in Japan because it allows for more space in a place where land is expensive. In Norway, couples generally sleep with their own single-size comforters though they share a double bed.

SLEEPING BUDDIES

One of the biggest differences across the world is whether people sleep communally or alone. Across Europe and North America, solo sleeping, or sleeping with just one partner, is the norm. But in Afghanistan, for example, all family members tend to sleep in the same room, which is then cleared of bedding during the day so the room can be used for other purposes. Indigenous Australians also sleep communally, often in rows, with the rows designed for overnight protection. Children and other vulnerable people sleep in the middle, with stronger adults on the ends.

SOCIAL AND SPIRITUAL SLEEPING

For many traditional people, sleep is a kind of temporary death, where we leave our bodies and touch the spirit world. Long sleeps are not especially desirable in these cultures, in case the soul wanders too far from the physical world and fails to return. The Gebusi people of Papua New Guinea avoid long, deep sleeps, and their men hold all-night seances every 11th night, where they chant and doze as they try to connect to the spirit world.

The Aché people of Paraguay also see sleep as quite a social activity. They sleep in huddles of mixed ages, alongside animals, and with hunters awake and active nearby. Unlike the Western sleep ideal, which is all about silence, darkness, and solitude, cultures like this see communal sleep as a kind of social bonding, where people can find safety and emotional reassurance among the community.

CELEBRATING THE NIGHT

The night isn't just a time for sleep, social bonding, or even work; it can also be a time of celebration. Let's look at some of the most interesting night celebrations from around the world.

HALLOWEEN

Perhaps the most famous celebration of the night, Halloween has its roots in a 2,000-year-old Celtic festival called Samhain, which means "summer's end" in Gaelic. Samhain was when the boundaries between our world and the spirit world blurred, so Celts would wear masks and costumes to confuse any evil spirits who wandered through from the other side.

When the festival was introduced in North America, orange and black became Halloween colors as orange represents harvest time (the autumn, when Halloween is celebrated) and black represents darkness and ending (like the ending of summer and the coming of dark winter nights). As for the association with bats, these are not only a symbol of witches, but also creatures that are attracted to open flames, like crackling bonfires, which may have originally been built to light the dead's way to the afterlife!

NEW YEAR'S EVE

Different cultures celebrate New Year's Eve on different days. However, December 31, the last night of the Gregorian calendar year, is a time for celebration in many corners of the globe. And everyone has different traditions to mark it.

In Denmark, people smash plates against doors; in Ecuador, they burn a paper-filled scarecrow; and in Switzerland, they drop ice cream on the floor. In Scotland, where New Year's Eve is called Hogmanay, there's a tradition called "first footing," where the first person to cross a house's threshold after midnight should be male, dark-haired, and carrying coal, shortbread, salt, and a black bun. Meanwhile, in many South American countries, the color of underwear a person sports on New Year's Eve is thought to influence the coming year, with yellow usually worn to bring luck, and red worn to bring love!

WAKAKUSA YAMAYAKI (BURNING MOUNTAIN FESTIVAL)

On one night every January in the ancient town of Nara in Japan, the Wakakusa Mountain blazes with a brilliant light, because the locals have enthusiastically set it on fire!

Why? One story says that the mountain was originally burned to get rid of rampaging wild boars that were destroying the mountain's temples. The other is that it was burned in a dispute between two neighboring landowners. Either way, it is now a joyful celebration that begins with a torch parade and doesn't end until the entire grass of the mountain is burned, which usually takes around an hour, but can go on all night in wet conditions!

WALPURGISNACHT

Legend has it that in Germany's Harz Mountains on the night of April 30 every year, witches and warlocks gather and fly to the range's highest peak to discuss their evil deeds.

While locals used to hang crosses and herbs on their doors to ward off the witches, Walpurgisnacht is now a time of celebration, and the night sky in the area is lit up with huge bonfires, whose dark clouds of smoke are said to be witches flying away and are greeted with a lot of cheering!

DIWALI

Diwali, the festival of light celebrated by Hindus, Sikhs, and Jains, might seem as if it doesn't belong in a book about the night. But not only is it about conquering darkness, its beautiful displays of colored lights and candles are made magical by the inky backdrop of the night sky.

This reminds us that, although we naturally crave light and the coming of a new day, these things are only what they are because their opposites, darkness and night, exist.

GOOD NIGHT!

The night is home not only to many fascinating myths and legends, but also to an amazing range of natural wonders. Its darkness isn't an echoing emptiness by any means. In fact, the night is a world as rich as the sunlit world we tend to inhabit.

There's no doubt that, wherever humans are found in the world, the night is changing, with light pollution and 24-hour living making their mark on ancient landscapes. There have also been some positive changes, for us at least, in that for most of us, the blackness of the night no longer means being hunted and eaten. While the night was once a scary black hole of the unknown, some parts of it are now familiar, thanks to science and technology — from the star-spangled sky spread out above our heads with its glowing Moon, to the dark waters beneath that reflect the Moon's pale light in their ripples.

While it's perfectly understandable that we have tried to light our way through the night's blackness, we are now in some danger of obliterating it. When we think about the difficulties we humans have with the extremes of midnight Sun and polar night, we should perhaps spare a thought for the birds chirping in confusion in sodium-lit city streets long before the Sun has begun to rise.

At the moment, we can still travel to Earth's most isolated spots, in deserts and on mountains, to see the jeweled wonders of the celestial sphere above our heads. But with 80% of us now living under light-polluted skies, we cannot take this for granted. Hopefully this book has shown you that the night is a magical place, and that switching off your lights at night to enjoy its magnificence is nothing to be afraid of.